GRUMPY CAT
COLORS THE WORLD
COLORING BOOK

ILLUSTRATIONS BY
Diego Jourdan Pereira

DOVER PUBLICATIONS, INC.
MINEOLA, NEW YORK

Grumpy Cat™

Illustrations by Diego Jourdan Pereira

Bibliographical Note

Grumpy Cat Colors the World Coloring Book, first published by Dover Publications, Inc., in 2016, contains the following previously published Dover books: *Grumpy Cat Hates Coloring* (2016) and *Grumpy Cat Vs. The World Coloring Book* (2016).

International Standard Book Number

ISBN-13: 978-0-486-81270-0
ISBN-10: 0-486-81270-7

Manufactured in the United States by RR Donnelley
81270701   2016
www.doverpublications.com

It's the face that has launched a thousand quips! Fans of the Internet sensation Grumpy Cat® can take a spin around the globe with the cranky feline in this delightful coloring book. It features sixty-two intricate full-page designs rendered in a rich mosaic style of the lovable sourpuss in traditional clothing and accessories. Of course, Grumpy Cat herself hates coloring books in general and this one in particular, but that's just why we love her! In addition, the pages are perforated and printed on one side only for easy removal and display.

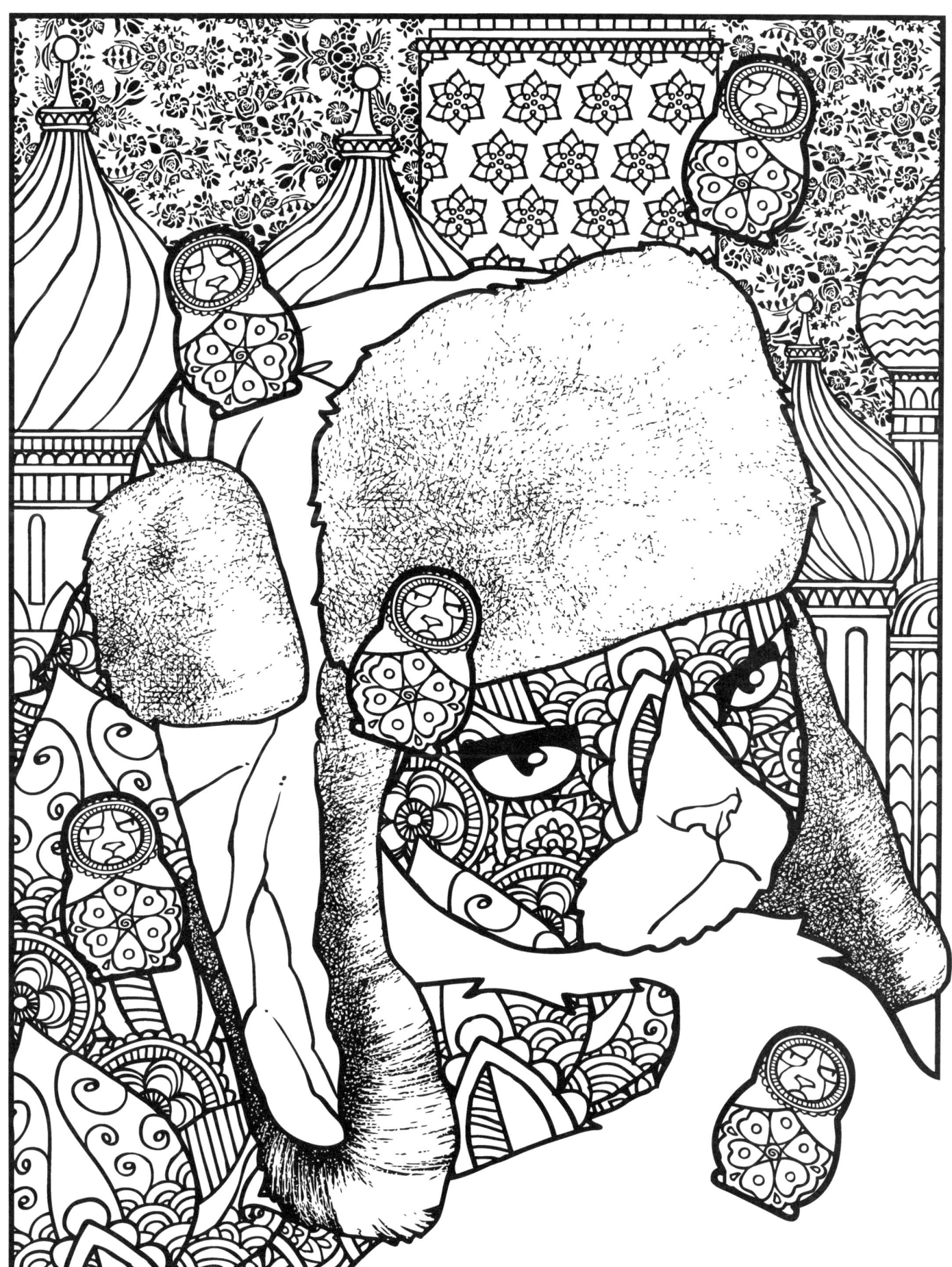

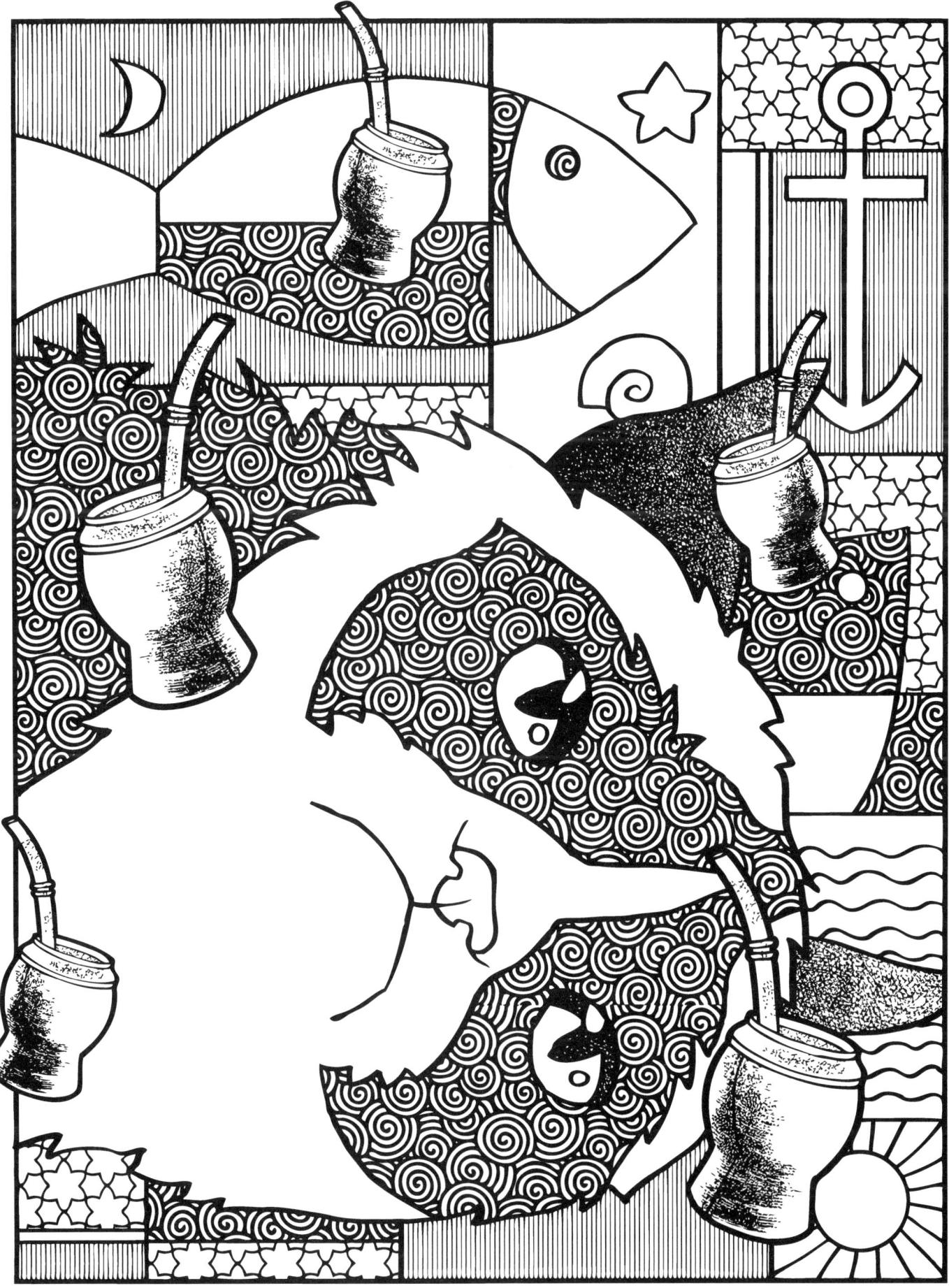

Laos

Panama

Fiji

Korea